Emerging Applications of Blockchain Technology

Develop a deeper understanding of emerging areas within the realm of blockchain "a disruptive technology".

SAURABH JAIN & VED PRAKASH BHARDWAJ

NOTION PRESS

NOTION PRESS

India. Singapore. Malaysia.

ISBN xxx-x-xxxxx-xx-x

This book has been published with all reasonable efforts taken to make the material error-free after the consent of the author. No part of this book shall be used, reproduced in any manner whatsoever without written permission from the author, except in the case of brief quotations embodied in critical articles and reviews.

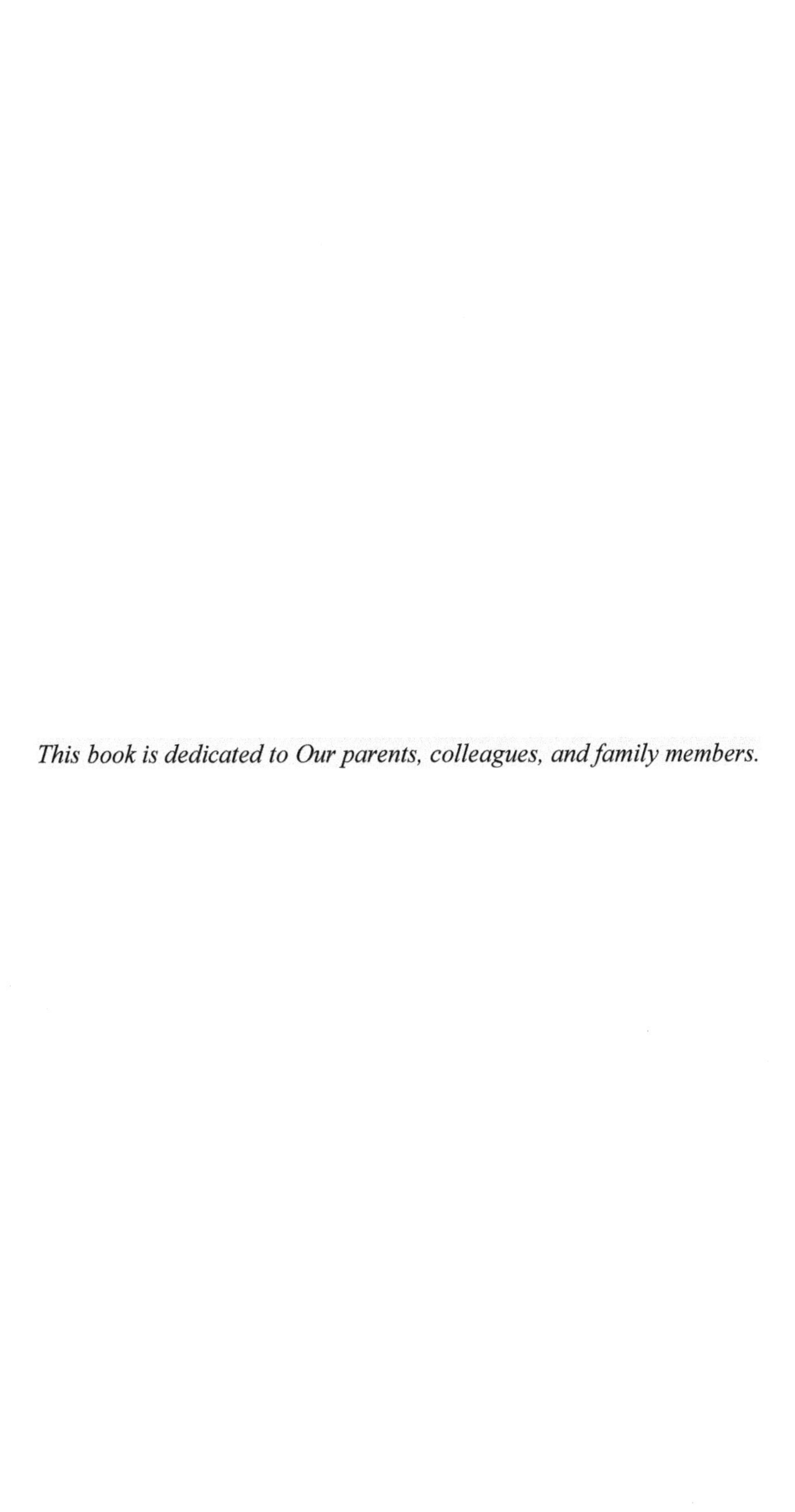

This book is dedicated to Our parents, colleagues, and family members.

Contents

CONTENTS

Preface

Currently, blockchain technologies are the most in-demand, and their adoption curve is just beginning. Several large corporations prioritise blockchain consolidation and other fields, including healthcare, education, supply chains, cybersecurity, the Internet of Things, etc. Multiple projects have begun utilising its implementations, solutions, and initiatives.

These guidelines can be used to create a blockchain and multiple solutions for emerging fields. This book will teach you the terms and ideas used in blockchain. The chapters of this book look at a number of new ways that blockchain technology is being used in the real world. Along with these informative chapters, this book also has case studies for putting blockchain-based applications into action.

Acknowledgements

We want to express our gratitude to our family members, for encouraging us to write books and sharing their valuable thoughts and experiences. This book could not have been complete without the support of our managers, colleagues and they inspired us to learn this technique and do research in this cutting-edge technology. Many thanks to our friends, colleagues, and students at the University of Petroleum and Energy Studies for their help and continued inspiration.

About Authors

Mr.Saurabh Jain has received a master's degree (M. Tech) in Information Security from MANIT, Bhopal, Madhya Pradesh, India, in 2012. He is pursuing his PhD in CSE from the University of Petroleum and Energy Studies, Dehradun, India. He has worked as an Assistant Professor in the Department of CSE at Oriental College of Technology, Bhopal. In the past, he has worked as HOD, M.Tech. Coordinator and Remote Center Coordinator in the Department of CSE at Oriental College of Technology, Bhopal, Madhya Pradesh, India, and currently working as Assistant Professor in the School of Computer Science at the University of Petroleum and Energy Studies, Dehradun. He has published 35+ international research papers, patents, and various book and book chapters. He has also organized several international/national conferences, workshops, FDPs, and STPs, and his research interest lies in network security, web security, cryptography and Blockchain technology.

Dr. Ved Prakash Bhardwaj is currently working as an Assistant Professor-Selection Grade in the School of Computer Science at the University of Petroleum and Energy Studies, Dehradun. He received his Ph.D. (CSE) and MTech (CSE) from the Jaypee University of Information Technology in 2014 and 2010, respectively. He received his B.E. (Computer Engineering) from Rajasthan University in 2008. Dr. Bhardwaj has published many papers in peer-reviewed Journals and Conferences of National and International repute with publishers like IEEE, ACM, Springer, Elsevier, etc. His primary area of research includes high-performance computing and machine learning.

List of Figures

1. History of Blockchain

The application of Blockchain technology is rapidly becoming a core component of our infrastructure!.

–Kevin Coleman

The history of blockchain should be understood by those who are passionate about the technology. Therefore, we have provided a thorough guide to Blockchain's history and evolution in order to help our readers learn about it and understand how it has changed over time.

Evolution of Blockchain

The idea of a blockchain was initially conceived by Stuart, Haber, and W. Scott Stornetta in the year 1991. They developed a cryptographically sound chain of blocks for their first project in order to prevent tampering with the timestamps of documents and ensure the integrity of the chain. In 1992, merkle trees were added to the system as part of the expansion. The efficiency of the system would increase if more papers could be kept on each block. However, in 2008, Satoshi Nakamoto's actions, or the work of a group that includes him, contributed to making the history of the blockchain more well-known.

It is generally agreed that Satoshi Nakamoto was the first person to develop the technology behind blockchains. Nakamoto is a relatively unknown character; yet, it is believed that he was the one who contributed to the development of Bitcoin, the first application of digital ledger technology.

Satoshi Nakamoto is credited with developing the very first blockchain in the year 2008. Since that time, the technology has progressed and been put to use for a wide range of reasons, including some that are unrelated to cryptocurrencies. The first first whitepaper on the subject was written by Satoshi Nakamoto in the year 2009. The fact that he stated in the whitepaper that the technology was decentralised gave the impression that no one person would ever be in charge of anything. Because of this, going this route is a good choice for boosting people's trust in online interactions.

Since Satoshi Nakamoto left the Bitcoin development team and passed the reins on to other key developers, the technology behind digital ledgers has advanced. As a direct consequence of this, new apps have been developed, which has contributed to the expansion of the blockchain.

The first Bitcoins were "mined" on January 3, 2009, when Satoshi Nakamoto used the code to create them. Because of this, the Bitcoin network started functioning properly. After a few days had passed, the initial transaction was finally finalised. In the months that followed, the number of people who used Bitcoin rapidly expanded, and on October 5, 2009, the first official exchange rate was established. An method that takes into consideration the cost of electricity necessary for a computer node to make a Bitcoin at the time determined that one Bitcoin, also known as BTC, was worth around $0.76 at the time (USD). As of the 7th of June, 2018, the value of one Bitcoin was around $7,693.50 USD. It reached a high of $19,783.06 US dollars. On February 6, 2010, the first day that individuals were finally able to buy and sell bitcoins on the recently formed dollar currency exchange. According to the website historyofbitcoin.org, the market capitalization of Bitcoin surpassed one million United States dollars within the same year and one billion United States dollars within three years as more people joined.

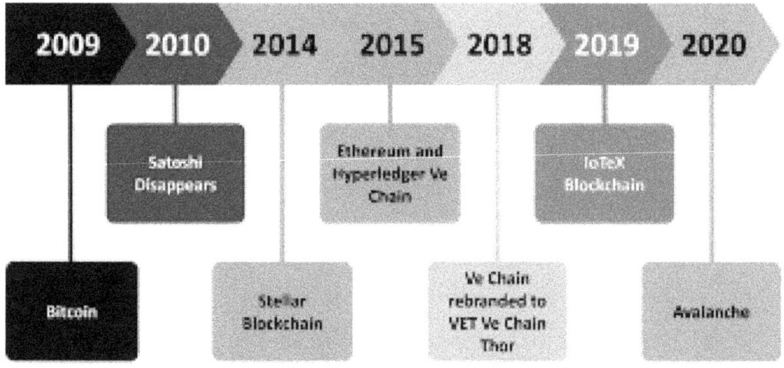

Figure 1 History of Blockchain Technology

Source: https://confirm.ie/2-history-of-blockchain/

First Evolutionary Stage (2008-2013)

Most people think that Bitcoin and Blockchain are the same thing. One is the technology behind most applications, including cryptocurrencies.

Bitcoin represented the initial application of the blockchain technology. In the whitepaper that he published in 2008, Satoshi Nakamoto refers to it as an online peer-to-peer network. Nakamoto was the one who created the genesis block, and all subsequent blocks were mined from that initial block. By connecting all of these blocks together, we were able to establish one of the longest information and transaction chains in the history of the entire globe.

Since the introduction of Bitcoin, which is based on blockchain technology, a profusion of new applications have emerged, each of which is aiming to take use of the tenets and promise of the digital ledger technology. Bitcoin is the first application to use blockchain technology. As a consequence of this, the history of blockchain offers a comprehensive list of applications for the technology as it has evolved.

Second Evolutionary Stage (2013-2015)

One of the original contributors to the Bitcoin codebase was Vitalik Buterin. He is one of a growing number of developers who believe that, in a world where innovation is the norm, Bitcoin has not yet realised all of the benefits of blockchain technology.

Buterin got the ball rolling on the development of what he thought would be a flexible blockchain that could function as more than just a P2P network. He was concerned about the limitations imposed by Bitcoin. In 2013, a new public blockchain known as Ethereum was released, and it had an expanded set of functionality compared to Bitcoin. This event marked a significant turning point in the history of the blockchain. To differentiate Ethereum from the Bitcoin Blockchain, Buterin developed a function that enables users to store non-contractual data, such as slogans. This addition was made. Due to the addition of this new feature, Ethereum is now capable of being utilised as a platform for the development of decentralised applications.

The Ethereum blockchain has become one of the most well-known applications of blockchain technology in the time since its formal launch in 2015. This launch occurred in 2015. This is due to the fact that it has the capability of supporting smart contracts, which have a wide variety of applications. In addition, the Ethereum blockchain technology has successfully attracted a thriving developer community, which has made the development of a genuine ecosystem much simpler. The majority of everyday transactions are processed over the Ethereum blockchain since it is capable of managing both smart contracts and decentralised applications. Additionally, the total market value of cryptocurrencies has seen tremendous growth.

Third Evolutionary Stage – Futures System

Bitcoin and Ethereum are just the beginning of the blockchain's history and development. In recent years, blockchain technology has been utilised in a number of projects. Attempts have been made by new projects to resolve some of the problems with Bitcoin and Ethereum while also creating brand-new blockchain-based features.

According to many accounts, NEO is the first open-source and decentralised blockchain platform to be developed in China. This programme runs on blockchain technology but is still rather young. In spite of the fact that cryptocurrencies are illegal in the country, new applications based on blockchain technology are still being developed. NEO, which is essentially the Chinese equivalent of Ethereum, is positioning itself to compete with Baidu in China. It has already received support from Jack Ma, who is the CEO of Alibaba.

IOTA came into being as a consequence of a brilliant proposal put up by a group of engineers to accelerate the expansion of the Internet of Things by utilising blockchain technology. Because it intends to provide distinctive verification processes and fee-free transactions, the cryptocurrency platform was developed specifically for the ecosystem of the Internet of Things. In addition to that, it addresses a few scaling issues that were present in Bitcoin Blockchain 1.0.

In addition to IOTA and NEO, there are a number of other second-generation blockchain platforms that are making waves in the business world. The blockchains Monero, Zcash, and Dash were built in attempt to solve some of the scalability and security issues that afflicted the early blockchain applications. These issues hampered the initial blockchain applications. The three distributed ledger platforms are together referred to as "privacy Altcoins" because they work toward the goal of making financial transactions as confidential and safe as possible.

In earlier iterations of this topic, we covered public blockchain networks as part of our history of blockchain talks. On a public blockchain network, all users have access to the data that is stored there. On the other hand, as technology advanced, an increasing number of businesses began to implement it in order to automate their procedures. Large firms often make major personnel investments in order to be on the cutting edge of technical innovation. Microsoft and Microsoft appear to be in the lead when it comes to researching the various applications that could be made possible by blockchain technology. Therefore, there are now such things as private blockchains, hybrid blockchains, and federated blockchains.

More information is available for interested readers here (References):
- *Blockchain history: https://101blockchains.com/history-of-blockchain-timeline/*
- *Van Mölken, R. (2018). Blockchain across Oracle: Understand the details and implications of the Blockchain for Oracle developers and customers. Packt Publishing Ltd.*
- *Nakamoto, S. (2008). Bitcoin: A peer-to-peer electronic cash system. Decentralized Business Review, 21260.*

2. Blockchain Technology for Insurance Sectors

"We have elected to put our money and faith in a mathematical framework that is free of politics and human error."
— Tyler Winkelvoss, Rower & Entrepreneur

The blockchain technology, which is often referred to as "distributed ledger technology," makes use of complex cryptographic methods to produce a safe record of data that cannot have anything added to it, altered about it, or removed from it without first having the appropriate authorization. Utilizing blockchain technology offers numerous benefits over utilising other technologies. The creation of an obvious audit trail and the maintenance of the confidentiality of the data are two of the most significant benefits. The use of a distributed ledger enables new methods for competitors to work together in a secure manner without the need to rely on third-party organisations. This is possible due to the immutability of blockchain systems and the absence of a requirement that they be monitored by a centralised authority. The following prerequisites have to be satisfied in figure number 2:

In spite of the widespread familiarity with blockchain's potential, insurance companies are still investigating the technology's applications inside their own organisations and throughout the insurance sector as a whole. A growing number of people are coming to the realisation that blockchain technology has the ability to radically transform the value chain of the insurance industry, making it safer, more efficient, less expensive, and more customer-friendly.

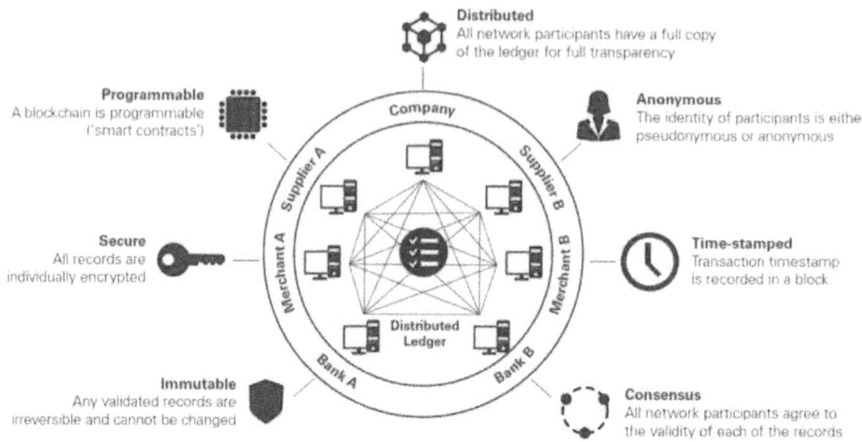

Figure 2:Blockchainand Insurance Sector

Image source: https://www.the-digital-insurer.com/how-blockchain-is-tackling-insurance-industry-challenges/

Blockchain technology will make it possible for a lot of different parties to send and receive data in a secure and verifiable way in real time. This will lead to a lot of efficiency gains, cost savings, more transparency, faster payouts, and less fraud. Blockchains can also help new insurance companies make better products and marketplaces. In a market where both consumers and businesses want the best deals and online experiences, there is a lot of competition among insurance companies. The insurance industry can change and grow with the help of blockchain technology.

Using Ethereum's smart contracts and decentralised applications, insurance transactions can be made through blockchain accounts. This allows for more automation and audit trails that can't be changed. Especially important is that the low cost of smart contracts and related transactions makes many products more competitive in the underdeveloped markets of developing countries.

Not to mention that the ecosystem that is growing around blockchain needs insurance. Cyber insurance can be used to get extra coverage like extensions and endorsements for financial loss (hot wallets and exchanges), currency and crime (cold wallets and vaults), professional liability (developers), and surety bonds (technology and software projects). Insurance companies can work with tech companies like ConsenSys Diligence to evaluate risk and get advice on how to manage and reduce losses.

Blockchain and warranties and records

- Create a record of the origin of a product that cannot be altered and that everyone can rely on as being accurate.

- Claims made about products can be investigated in real time, even from other countries' perspectives.

- By enhancing data and the manner in which data is exchanged, you can lend a hand to the industry as a whole in its fight against claim fraud.

Blockchian and KYC and AML

- Utilizing blockchain technology, it is possible to create a safe database of customer information that is also mobile.

- This approach of working together lessens the likelihood of making mistakes and prevents individuals from performing the same tasks several times, which economises both time and resources.

- Ensure that all institutions have access to the information regarding what customers are doing to increase regulatory oversight and compliance.

Blockchain and insurance policies parameters

- Put the logic of a policy into a smart contract, and then when a preset loss event takes place, let an oracle, which is a digital feed, take over and run the contract.

- There should be no assistance from other persons required in the settling and clearing of any deals.

- It is essential to simplify the understanding of insurance-linked securities such as crop insurance, insurance for aircraft delays and cancellations, and any others that may be relevant (ILS).

Blockchain technology and reinsurance sector

- Blockchain technology makes it possible for various parties, including brokers, regulators, reinsurers, and primary insurers, to exchange data in a secure manner and in real time.

- All three of these tasks—risk modelling, compliance audits, and risk assessments—can be carried out in an automated fashion.

- Establish a connection between a variety of risk and treaty towers and a time-stamped smart contract.

Blockchain technology and claim process

- Create a record of claims that can be relied on by everyone and that cannot be altered in any way.

- It is necessary to break down the data silos in order to put an end to persons making misleading claims.

- Customers should be given greater access to their data and more choice over how it is used.

Blockchain affect on insurance distribution

- It would be cost effective to save money by coordinating the activities of several participants in an online marketplace.

- Users of the platform should have the ability to manage a large number of policies and have direct access to a large number of providers.

- Make premium or claim payment transactions simple, quick, and inexpensive.

Blockchaina and peer-to-peer (P2P) insurance

- Using blockchain technology, peer-to-peer (P2P) structures such as mutuals and reciprocals can be improved by automating chores and putting money in escrow on smart contracts.

- To facilitate policyholder alignment and provide incentives, emerging P2P networks make use of tokens and token staking.

Examples of Blockchain in the Insurance Industry

According to Gartner, blockchain technology will reach critical mass by the year 2023, and as a result, the value of firms would increase by $3.1 trillion by the year 2030. At this point, the estimations are valuable enough to warrant the time and effort that you spent into developing them.

Already, the field of insurance is teeming with brilliant businesspeople and platforms that create a significant amount of value using blockchain technology. Consider some persuasive instances.

IBM

IBM was established in 1911.

Location: Armonk,New York

The work that IBM is doing on Blockchain makes a number of procedures in the insurance industry more straightforward. As a result of this study, this company has assisted other businesses in the insurance industry in the process of automating their underwriting and claims systems. As a result of these changes, turnaround times and the number of fraudulent claims have decreased, which has helped insurers earn the trust of their consumers and provide them with more dependable service.

Countrywide

Began in 1925

Location: Columbus

Even though Nationwide Insurance has been in the industry of providing insurance for quite some time, the company is still dedicated to expanding through the use of blockchain technology. Not only did the corporation become a member of the RiskBlock Alliance, but it was also the pioneering organisation to implement the blockchain technology that had been developed by the alliance. By utilising the platform's quicker and more secure assistance with proof of insurance, customers are able to rapidly verify their information with law enforcement and begin the process of filing a claim.

Deloitte

Establised in 1845

Location: New York City

Deloitte assists its customers in the incorporation of cutting-edge technology into their workplaces by informing insurance businesses about blockchain. Following research into health and life insurance, the company came to the conclusion that it could utilise blockchain technology to not only discover false claims but also store medical records, conduct business using smart contracts, and make transactions. Therefore, by utilising Deloitte's blockchain solutions, insurance firms have the ability to better their interactions with their customers and patients.

Lemonade

In 2015, the production of the fourth batch of lemonade.

Location: New York City

Lemonade provides renters insurance beginning at $5 per month and homeowners insurance beginning at $25 per month, respectively. AI and technology that uses distributed ledgers are utilised in order to do this. Smart contracts are utilised alongside blockchain technology. In accordance with the strategic plan for the organisation, a predetermined fee is deducted from each monthly payment, and the remaining funds are allocated to cover pending claims. In the event that a claim is submitted, the smart contracts stored on the blockchain will make every effort to validate the client's loss as quickly as is practically possible in order to reimburse them.

Etherisc

Established in 2016

Location: Remote

Etherisc is an open-source platform that allows developers to construct insurance applications without the need for a centralised server. The blockchain technology is utilised in the production of decentralised software for the insurance industry by the company. Utilizing ledger technology to reduce inefficiencies such as high processing costs and prolonged claim processing times is the primary objective of this initiative.

B3I

Established in 2016

Location: Remote

In order to investigate the potential applications of blockchain and distributed ledger technology within the insurance business, a consortium of insurance companies came together to form the Blockchain Insurance Industry Initiative, often known as B3i. The company was established in 2016, and its mission statement is that it intends to leverage blockchain technology to make it simpler to manage data and payments, as well as to cut risk and insurance costs. The B3i programme implements a full digital transformation of the reinsurance process in order to make it more efficient.

Dynamis

start up in 2006

Location: Virginia

Mutual insurance between individuals or businesses The construction of Dynamis makes exclusive use of the Ethereum blockchain. It focuses mostly on unemployment benefits, also referred to as "social capital," which are discussed throughout. The applicant's LinkedIn profile is all that is required in order to perform the policy-required check on the applicant's present employment. A person's profile links will be examined by the blockchain of the organisation to determine whether or not they are unemployed before the individual may receive insurance benefits.

Smart Contract for Banking System

Platform used for smart contract deployment is etherum remix. Ethereum remix can be accessed by using this link http://remix.ethereum.org/

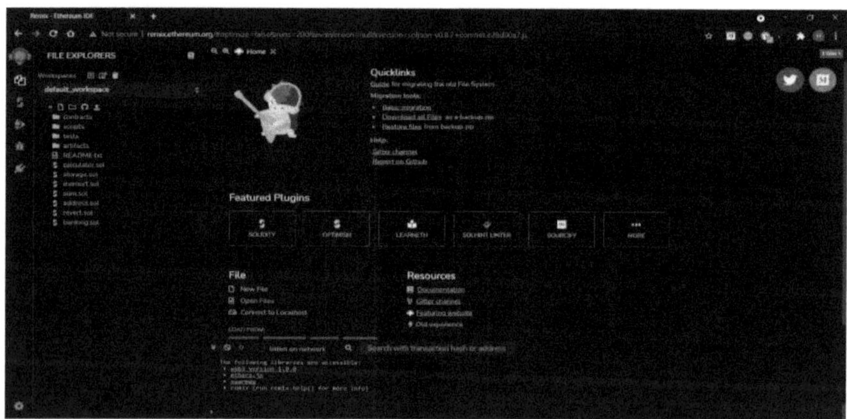

Writing the smart contract for banking system and compile it and deploy it on remix etherum platform.

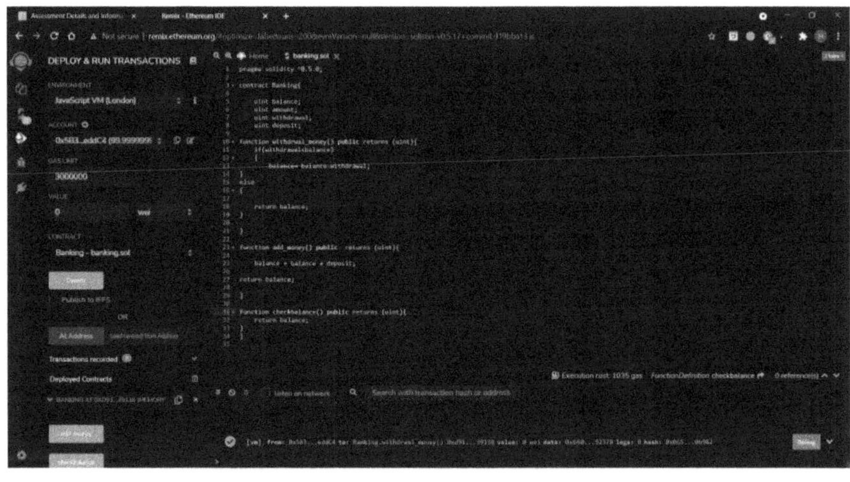

Readers interested in learning more can do so by visiting the following links (References) :

https://consensys.net/blockchain-use-cases/finance/insurance/
https://builtin.com/blockchain/blockchain-insurance-companies

3. Blockchain Technology for Agriculture

Agriculture is our wisest pursuit, because it will, in the end, contribute most to real wealth, good morals, and happiness.

—Thomas Jefferson

The introduction of blockchain technology has made it feasible to obtain data that has been validated, which has the effect of making users more trustworthy. The blockchain is able to record and monitor each stage, from a product's inception all the way through its final disposal, that is included in its value chain. For the purpose of developing data-driven facilities and insurance solutions that will make farming more intelligent and less prone to risk, obtaining reliable data from the farming process is highly vital.

Blockchain and Agriculture

Everyone adds the details of their own accounts and transactions to the distributed ledger, which is where the data is stored. When it comes to agriculture, it can be difficult and expensive to obtain information about farms, inventories, and contracts; however, this service promises to be a trustworthy source of such details. The blockchain technology makes it possible to monitor the supply chain of food. Consumers will have more faith as a result of the increased ease with which they can trust food supply chains. It is a dependable method of storing data, and as a result, it encourages the use of data-driven technology to make farming more intelligent. When coupled with smart contracts, this technology also makes it possible for payments to be made between parties whenever there is a change in the data stored in the blockchain. This article explores the potential applications of blockchain technology in the food supply chain, agricultural insurance, intelligent farming, and the purchase and sale of agricultural products. We also discuss how difficult it is to maintain tabs on the financial dealings of small-scale farmers and the steps that need to be taken to establish an ecosystem for the application of blockchain technology in the food and agriculture industries.

People are able to conduct trustworthy transactions with one another through the use of blockchain technology, which eliminates the need for a third party intermediary such as a bank for cryptocurrency or a middleman in the agriculture industry. Because technology eliminates the requirement for a centralised authority, it has the potential to alter the process through which trust is bestowed. People now rely on cryptography and architecture that is peer-to-peer rather than on authorities to keep their data secure. Therefore, by helping to rebuild confidence between producers and customers, it contributes to a reduction in the expenses associated with conducting business in the agri-food sector.

The blockchain technology makes it simple to record and verify transactions between parties that are not personally known to one another. Therefore, it is simple to identify instances of fraud and errors. Inaccuracies can also be reported in real time when using smart contracts, which is another benefit of this technology. This makes it much simpler to locate things in the extensive supply chain, which is particularly helpful given the complexity of the agriculture and food production system. Therefore, technology provides explanations for the concerns that individuals, governments, and other organisations have regarding the quality and safety of food.

Farming that is both astute and productive

All forms of agriculture are founded on the facts and knowledge that we have accumulated regarding our natural resources, and agri-food systems are no exception. Products go through a number of processes that increase their value as they flow from input to output, whereas data, information, and money move in the reverse direction. Different actors and stakeholders generate and make use of data and information in accordance with the requirements they have and the capabilities they possess. Information and communication technology (ICT), the internet of things (IoT), and a multitude of novel ways to collect and analyse data, including as unmanned aerial vehicles (UAV), sensors, and machine learning, are all utilised by smart agriculture. Building a smart agriculture infrastructure requires a number of steps, one of which is the installation of a comprehensive security system that simplifies data use and management. Because traditional methods of handling data are centralised, they are susceptible to cyberattacks, faulty data, data distortion, and misuse of the information. The data collected from monitoring the environment are managed by government bodies with vested interests the vast majority of the time. They are able to sway people's opinions by presenting them with evidence.

The blockchain technology is used to store data and information that is created by a variety of different parties and stakeholders at every stage of the agricultural production process, from the seed to the sale of the final product. It guarantees that none of the information that has been recorded can be altered and that all of the data and information may be accessed by anyone who has a requirement for them. When data is distributed to the personal computers of stakeholders rather from being stored on servers that are managed centrally by administrators, the risk of data corruption or loss is significantly reduced. A blockchain is a type of database that maintains a record of timestamps for various groupings of transactions and activities that are associated with a certain product. It is much less probable for data to be lost or altered when it is delivered to servers that are managed by the internet, as opposed to when it is held on servers that are overseen by administrators. Creating mobile applications for agriculture that are powered by data is made much easier with the help of the database. A complete and safe infrastructure for the Internet of Things (IoT) may also be built with the help of the blockchain, which also helps bring together various forms of information and communications technology (ICT) used in e-agriculture.

Infrastructure for the Provision of Food

The food supply chains have become longer and more intricate as a direct result of the expansion of globalisation and the increased level of competition in the market. Traceability of food, food safety and quality, trust in food, and inefficient supply chains are typical issues in food supply networks that pose a threat to society, the economy, and people's health. Traceability of food is very important.

Companies can utilise blockchain technology to increase customer trust in their products and improve the reputations of those products by including accurate information about those products in the blockchain. Increasing the value of a company's products is one way for that company to become more competitive. Because of this, dishonest and low-quality merchants would have a difficult time remaining in business, and this would force all sellers in the agriculture and food industries to improve the quality of their products. The blockchain offers consumers information that is precise and trustworthy regarding the cultivation and distribution of food products. This is seen from the perspective of the consumer. It makes individuals feel better about the quality, safety, and environmental friendliness of the food that they buy. Those who buy organic food are more likely to feel this way. The usage of blockchain makes it simpler for customers and producers to communicate with one another, which in turn assists individuals in gaining a deeper understanding of the processes involved in the production of food. Customers have an easier time trading things with one another, which in turn builds their ties with one another and their belief in the safety of food. From the perspective of regulatory agencies, blockchain technology provides them with precise and trustworthy data, which assists them in formulating rules that are effective.

The blockchain is able to keep track of the history of a product, from the location where it was manufactured to the locations where it was sold. The information that is gathered at the beginning of the supply chain, such as the DNA of livestock animals or the amount of pesticides that are still on grains and vegetables, can be stored in a secure manner for an extended period of time using this technology. Any business that is a part of the product's supply chain has the ability to verify this information and ensure that it is accurate. Finding out information of this nature about each product can be time-consuming and expensive; nevertheless, samples might be of assistance. This type of information can be put to use to locate meat that hasn't been disclosed, as was the case in 2013 when Europe encountered an issue with horse meat.

There have been several ideas developed to simplify the process of tracing the origin of agricultural products, and a significant number of these proposals make use of blockchain technology. Radio Frequency Identifying (RFID), which is an automatic identification and communication technology that does not require physical touch, might be used to develop a system for tracking food as it moves through the supply chain. This would be possible because to RFID's usage of wireless technology. It is able to use trustworthy data to track the whereabouts of products along the supply chain. By utilising blockchain technology, one can ensure that the records of manufacturing, processing, storage, and distribution are accurate.

Traceability using Blockchain

The food supply chain has become significantly more global over the course of the past few years. The importance of farm-to-fork food safety and quality certification has increased as a direct result of this development. It is more important than ever to have a cutting-edge traceability system, which is a key quality control tool that ensures products in the food supply chain are safe. This is because threats to food safety and contamination are getting worse, and because of this, it is more important than ever to have a traceability system.

It is common knowledge that India has a massive population, which translates to a massive amount of untapped potential for growth and success in the food industry. In the not-too-distant future, it is anticipated that India will overtake the United States to become the nation with the highest GDP. While this is happening, the agricultural sector of India, which accounts for approximately 13.7% of the country's gross domestic product and employs approximately half of the country's workforce, is seeing a decline. In recent times, concerns concerning the availability of food have garnered a lot of attention. One of the industries that brings in a lot of money is the one that deals with the supply chain for food all over the world. According to the scenario, there are issues occurring with the supply chain. According to the findings of an inquiry that took place in December of 2017, 65 of the 72 food testing facilities that were under the supervision of the Food Safety and Standards Authority of India (FSSAI) were operating illegally. Because they were not complying with the Food Safety and Standards Act of 2006, well-known food delivery services such as Zomato, Swiggy, and Meals Panda ceased their services in October 2018, preventing them from delivering food to 10,500 hotels and restaurants (FSS Act). In addition, some establishments lacked the fundamental government certifications required by food safety controllers. The majority of India's urban areas had food service enterprises, particularly restaurants, that served their patrons stale food. Not very long ago, a well-known chocolate manufacturer discovered that their product contained pieces of plastic. Lead, which is hazardous to one's health, was found to be present in one of the most common varieties of noodles. Because of the growing number of food recalls that take place every year all over the world, food manufacturers and distributors are forced to pay an ever-increasing amount of money to carry out recalls. It is difficult to track food from the farm to the consumer's plate, which is why mistakes are more expensive. It is becoming increasingly vital, in addition to keeping an eye on the components, to keep an eye on and control the wallets of the consumers. This is because being able to observe how things are done is essential to maintaining a high level of food safety. It should now be able, as a result of recent modifications to the food traceability management system (TMS), to trace the quality and safety of food from the moment it is farmed until the time it is consumed. 11 million people around the world lose their lives each year as a direct result of not having enough food to consume. That accounts for one death in every five that occur over the entire world. Both traditional procedures and those in use today are incapable, on their own, of providing traceability from beginning to end.

Using the technology behind blockchains, one might be able to find a solution to this issue. It is now possible to trace the origin of food in real time, which has significant positive implications for the wellbeing of the individuals who consume the food in question. Tracking and management of agricultural products is now possible thanks to blockchain technology. This ensures that all participants in the supply chain, from farmers to merchants, have access to the maximum amount of information. A person who sells mutton is aware of when an animal is killed, when the meat is shipped, how long it takes to ship, how long it can be consumed before it goes bad, and how long it takes to ship. Using this information, the retailer will be able to monitor the progress of the goods as it moves through the supply chain in real time. One should also be aware of the risk of getting sick from the diet. By doing so, medical professionals are able to more rapidly diagnose a sick individual by referring to the most fundamental information about the food item in question. This helps save lives in addition to resources. Traceability ensures that customers and their clients who pay more for goods that are certified as organic and free of GMOs receive high-quality goods that meet their needs. Customers who pay more for goods that are certified as organic and free of GMOs are also more likely to pay more for these goods. Because it eliminates the need for intermediaries, blockchain technology makes it possible for merchants and farmers to communicate and engage with one another directly. This results in increased revenue and profits for both groups. This arrangement might have a significant impact on the smaller farmers that sell their produce to the neighbourhood shops. If the blockchain is able to determine that a merchant has run out of potatoes, a neighbouring farmer will be able to immediately provide the merchant with potatoes to cover the gap. Because of blockchain technology, the transaction can take place without the need for a phone call or an online order form. The farmer claims that there are not enough potatoes, but he alters the distributed ledger to make it appear as though they will be able to satisfy the demand. Because of the latest update to the blockchain, the merchant has indicated that they are now willing to take the potatoes. Small farmers may find it easier to break into new markets with the assistance of local companies and markets. Performance will drastically improve and needs will be addressed with far more precision if blockchain technology is used to replace a significant number of the procedures in the negotiating phase. One of these technologies is used to make the livestock supply chain less dependent on the utilisation of a centralised network. This not only broadens the exposure that field commodities receive on the market, but it also makes it simpler for sellers and producers to do their work more quickly and rake in more revenue.

Recent years have seen significant shifts in the food industry, despite the fact that some challenges were encountered. One of these issues is networks of procedures, items, and data that are difficult to comprehend due to the fact that they do not communicate with one another. When there is insufficient transparency, it can be difficult to determine what costs are reasonable and what a product's level of quality actually is. The use of data in agriculture is necessary because of regulations imposed by the government, fraud, and the current state of the food supply. Customers and merchants now have a forum to discuss prices openly thanks to blockchain technology. Instead than going via shops or any other kind of middleman, distributors are now able to pay their clients directly. People don't have to worry about their money being stolen when they transmit it to their agricultural partners in other nations. A supply chain can benefit from blockchain technology by becoming more transparent and straightforward. More people will be aware of food safety issues and take action as a result of the ease with which all of the information regarding the origin of the food can be located. The customer's needs are met in every aspect, from the creation and management of digital IDs to the processing of payments. In the twenty-first century, solutions based on blockchain technology are the key to growth that is beneficial to all parties involved. It is difficult to identify strong business models and intriguing uses for blockchain technology, despite the fact that it has the ability to solve major challenges in the food and agriculture industries in a more efficient manner. This is because blockchain technology is based on a distributed ledger. Many people believe that in the not-too-distant future, the blockchain technology will play a significant part in the agricultural industry. As part of their exhaustive and in-depth research into the potential applications of blockchain technology in the agricultural sector, the innovation specialists on our team visited more than 150 different farm operations.

Challenges in Agriculture

Even ten years ago, the agricultural industry was experiencing prosperous times. On the other hand, as the procedure becomes more involved, a variety of issues are starting to become apparent. They have already slowed down the chain of persons who provide food to people because they are concentrating on the wrong things. Therefore, blockchain technology is more crucial than it has ever been in this industry. Let's check into the following, shall we?

The upcoming trends in consumer behaviour

The ever-shifting tastes of consumers are one of the industry's most intractable challenges. As a result, different materials have distinct requirements. Because the majority of farmers make their living off of a single crop, they are in a challenging situation right now. In most cases, individuals will select only a single variety of vegetable. As a result of shifts in demand, customers may either receive a substantial reward or a very modest return on their investment. In general, it's stressful, and a lot of farmers have to learn to accept the fact that if they lose money, they have to go on to other things. They are unable to plan for how the problem will affect them in their day-to-day life, so it has an effect on them.

Competitiveness of Goods and Services

There are many different stores from which we may purchase the stuff we require on a daily basis. There is always a great deal of danger involved due to the fact that they are the most sought after. Therefore, it is difficult for smaller farmers to compete in marketplaces that are controlled by monopolistic multinational giants like corporations.

This widens the divide between large corporations and individual farmers, as individual farmers are unable to enter the system without risking the risk of their business failing, despite the fact that the food they produce is superior to that produced by market leaders. In addition, and as is typically the case, a great number of farmers and small enterprises lack the resources necessary to market their products, which hastens the process of their extinction.

Insufficient handling of the inventory

Because the majority of the items in this sector are raw materials, effective inventory management is of the utmost significance. As a result, it does not go through any procedures that would help it last for a longer period of time. Everything, from plants to flesh, will eventually become rancid. Therefore, before pushing forward with the sale, they need to be certain that their stock is adequately protected.

However, a significant number of agricultural operations do not possess the resources necessary to effectively manage their supplies. It's possible that this will result in wasted time, effort, and materials. To add insult to injury, the farmers would suffer financial losses as a direct result of this. In spite of their best efforts, they are unable to sell the goods because they are unable to effectively manage the stock that they have.

The underutilised use of technology

The fact that technology and automation are not utilised to their full potential in this sector is another issue that has to be addressed. In point of fact, the majority of farmers do not have the financial resources necessary to purchase pricey farming equipment or machinery. As a result of the rapid pace at which the world is undergoing change and the significant strides that have been made in terms of technological advancement, a variety of farming technologies have been developed to assist farmers.

On the other side, farmers fall behind the times because they are unable to obtain the necessary funds or do not have sufficient knowledge regarding this technology. In order to continuously increase their productivity, large agricultural corporations consistently implement cutting-edge technologies. On the other hand, it is impossible for small and medium-sized firms to proceed in the same manner.

Restrictions imposed by the government

In order to preserve the harmony of the planet, laws have been enacted. However, a nation's constraints on agriculture shouldn't have an adverse effect on the amount of food that nation produces. Many firms are unsuccessful as a direct result of the stringency of some government regulations as well as the significant increase in taxation on all fronts.

In example, stringent regulations typically make it difficult for agricultural production to advance. We are not suggesting that the government should have zero involvement in the industry in any way, shape, or form. But undermining the potential of a large company by acting in an excessive manner is never a good idea.

Expansion demands large land costs

The cost of available farmland is highly volatile and does not remain stable for long. Land prices appear to fluctuate frequently due to the fact that there is an inadequate supply of money on the market. The cost of land is typically too high to allow for expansion to be feasible. In addition to this, there is not always a large quantity of land available. Numerous companies and farmers are put in a difficult financial position as a result of the increased taxes that are associated with the purchase of huge tracts of land.

Therefore, even if a farmer or business is successful, they won't be able to expand enough to satisfy the requirements of the market.

Infrastructure failures

For a variety of causes, the infrastructure necessary for farming in rural regions is deteriorating at a moderate but steady rate. Natural disasters, declining soil fertility, and rapid urbanisation are all potential reasons of this trend. Because some of the components are not in sync with the infrastructure, it might be challenging to keep things going in a manner that is sustainable. The failure of modernization to function properly in this region also contributes to the breakdown of the infrastructure, which in turn causes further losses.

It is possible for difficulties such as these to arise even in huge organisations if there are not sufficient support structures in place. For their operations to be successful, businesses of any kind require basic necessities such as money, land, and roadways. However, if necessary components aren't readily available, the operation can be put in jeopardy.

Farming should be done in a safe and secure manner. The problem of farm safety is one that should not be overlooked. On every farm, there are either animals, machinery, or vehicles that can assist in the transportation of goods. However, if the criminals manage to get access to your property, they can take your animals or your machines with them. Theft is a common problem in the agricultural industry, but farmers struggle to combat it because they lack the tools necessary to protect their property.

Therefore, even if they are able to purchase sophisticated equipment, they will still need to invest additional money to ensure that they are secure. Additionally, there are not many options to safeguard farmers in the manner in which they require protection at this time.

Blockchain in Agriculture–advantages

Agriculture is another wealthy industry that can benefit substantially from the use of blockchain technology and its characteristics. Let's have a look at the primary advantages of this market area.

Agricultural Stock Management

In truth, many farming businesses lack the funds needed to deploy cutting-edge stock management systems. This could result in a waste of both resources and products. Not to mention the financial stress this situation places on farmers. As a result, it places a great strain on farmers who lack the resources necessary to effectively handle the situation.

However, by implementing blockchain technology in agricultural situations, they will be able to permanently transform that condition. The management of supplies and stocks is one area where blockchain excels. As a result, it may be highly beneficial to farmers to keep their stocks in good condition. The truth is that blockchain technology can monitor storage facility conditions and alert consumers when perishable items are about to expire. As a result, you'll be able to take the essential precautions.

Productivity of the Agricultural Supply Chain

Another intriguing application of blockchain technology in this business is the possibility for enhanced agricultural efficiency. The main reason this sector's efficiency falls short of expectations is that neither automation nor technology are fully utilised. In fact, smaller and medium-sized farmers are more likely to lack access to pricey technologies that may otherwise boost the total output of their operations.

As a result, blockchain technology can surely be beneficial in this regard. It can manage all elements immediately, lower the cost of agricultural activities, and boost the overall efficiency of the output by employing an immutable ledger system built on blockchain technology.

Modernization of Farm Management Software

Another advantage of blockchain technology for agriculture is the process of modernising farm management software. In fact, farm management software will become extensively employed in a relatively short amount of time. Despite this, the programme remains based on the classic client-server approach. As a result, they are still unable to generate as much as they could if blockchain technology was implemented. As a result, utilising blockchain technology in this case can assist in elevating the FMS to a whole new level. Blockchain protection will also ensure that this programme has the necessary level of security. Farmers will not have to worry about being hacked as a result.

IoT devices are necessary in the agricultural industry to ensure proper inventory control. Agriculture IoT Optimization Security Furthermore, these systems can provide some level of safety and protection for their equipment. They can use the gadgets to monitor the state of the land and the weather, and then make any necessary adjustments. Furthermore, some of these technologies are capable of predicting natural calamities. Nonetheless, these devices are now extremely vulnerable to attack. It's an issue because many of the cloud services they employ to store data are vulnerable to cyberattacks. As a result, the level of security varies greatly. However, blockchain technology may be able to assist in this situation. Using blockchain technology in agriculture would improve the networking infrastructure to which Internet of Things devices have access while also ensuring their security. Blockchain technology has the potential to benefit a wide range of other industries. To learn more about blockchain technology, visit our detailed description of its different benefits.

Maintaining Reasonable Prices

It is true that many agricultural firms do not receive the fair pricing for their produce that they believe they should. Many wholesalers continue to underpay farmers and ranchers for their labour in growing crops and raising animals. In reality, most farmers acquire only the minimal needs to ensure their survival.

As a result, if blockchain technology is applied to agriculture, the dynamic may change. They may sell their items to trustworthy customers and perhaps reach more people than they did previously owing to a marketplace enabled by blockchain technology. As a result, they will be better prepared to bargain over prices. Farmers will be able to receive the full remuneration they deserve in this manner.

Sharing of Agricultural Subsidies

However, it is ultimately our responsibility to pay for the agricultural subsidies. Even if it is paid for by the government, the budget for the money comes from the taxes we pay. However, there is zero transparency when it comes to the subsidies. Additionally, bias is frequently visible, with larger organisations frequently obtaining more than they need while smaller farms frequently do not receive enough to meet their needs.

As a result, the introduction of blockchain technology in the agriculture industry may aid in increasing the level of transparency surrounding this critical issue. The public may examine whether or not the money is being given to the proper farmers by the government using a public blockchain to transfer subsidies to the relevant farmers.

Providing Microloans to Farmers

Another fantastic use of blockchain technology in the agricultural industry is the ability to receive microloans. In fact, small- to medium-sized farms frequently need financial support in the form of loans in order to maintain their operations. The interest rates that banks charge on loans, on the other hand, are significantly higher.

The enterprises are consequently in a hard position because the interest rates may force them to take out extra loans. As a result, adopting blockchain technology to this problem might offer a long-term fix. The blockchain network may make it simpler for individuals to receive microloans from global lenders. If they take out a lesser loan as the interest rates would be more affordable, they will be able to maintain the firm for a longer period of time.

Agriculture- Blockchain based Startups

Following are the emerging companies based that work on the growth of agriculture industry.

AgriChain

It is a firm that uses blockchain technology with the goal of eliminating the need for middlemen by enabling farmers to process and transact business with one another.

AgriDigital

It is an integrated system for the management of goods on the global grains market that is based on blockchain technology. By utilising digital contracts, the platform makes it simpler to handle the many complex financial aspects of agricultural operations.

AgriLedger

It is a social entrepreneurship project headquartered in the United Kingdom that aims to assist farmers in improving their access to funding, tracking transactional data, and learning more about the origin of the food they produce.

Demeter

It is a central hub that eliminates the need for middlemen, cumbersome processes, and expensive fees by providing anyone with the ability to rent and cultivate microfields anywhere in the world.

Etherisc

It is a blockchain firm that provides decentralised insurance apps to farmers so that they can purchase crop insurance.

Ripe

This startup is constructing the Blockchain of Food by establishing a transparent digital food supply chain and making use of data that is of a high quality.

TE-FOOD

This company monitors fresh food, animals, and transportation along the supply chain using various tracking systems.

Worldcovr

It is a firm that provides crop insurance to protect farmers from the risk of losing their crops. In order to do this, the company monitors rainfall using satellites and pays out the farmers as promptly as possible.

There is a fair possibility that the market for the development of agricultural blockchains will be a significant one. It is anticipated that the market for agricultural blockchain technology will expand at a rate of 47.8% annually, rising from an estimated $41.2 million in 2017 to more than $430 million in 2023. (CAGR).Already, blockchain technology is revolutionising the business by reducing the likelihood of fraudulent activity, accelerating the pace of transactions, assisting farmers in caring for and keeping track of their crops, and a great deal more.

References:

- *H. Xiong, T. Dalhaus, P. Wang, and J. Huang, "Blockchain Technology for Agriculture: Applications and Rationale," Front. Blockchain, vol. 3, 2020.*
- *D. Prashar, N. Jha, S. Jha, Y. Lee, and G. P. Joshi, "Blockchain-based traceability and visibility for agricultural products: A decentralized way of ensuring food safety in India," Sustainability, vol. 12, no. 8, p. 3497, 2020.*
- *S. Insights, "8 Blockchain startups disrupting the agricultural industry," StartUs Insights, 19-Dec-2018. [Online]. Available: https://www.startus-insights.com/innovators-guide/8-blockchain-startups-disrupting-the-agricultural-industry/*

4. Blockchain For Healthcare Industry

For the foreseeable future, I'm all about building blockchain-based decentralized services.

— Fred Ehrsam

Blockchain in healthcare

Blockchain is a relatively new technology that is being utilised in a variety of different industries, including the healthcare industry, to develop novel approaches to completing certain tasks. The healthcare business makes use of a blockchain network to facilitate the storage and transmission of patient information between various entities, including hospitals, diagnostic labs, pharmaceutical companies, and individual doctors. Blockchain technology has the potential to identify significant errors in the medical industry, some of which could be fatal. Therefore, it has the potential to make the process of sharing medical data across the healthcare business simpler, safer, and more open. By utilising this technology, medical institutions are able to improve their patient analysis as well as their ability to understand more about their patients.

Healthcare needs blockchain

Concerning problems with medical care, it is important for technology to improve quickly. In today's world, there is a growing need for high-quality medical facilities with cutting-edge technology. In this case, Blockchain would be the only way for the healthcare industry to change. Also, the healthcare industry is reorganising itself to focus on a patient-centered strategy, with a special focus on two important factors: how easy it is to get services and how many medical resources are always available. Because healthcare organisations use blockchain technology, they can offer better medical facilities and care for their patients. Health Information Exchange is a repetitive process that takes a lot of time and adds to the cost of health care. But with the help of technology today, the same problems can be solved much more quickly. People can take part in many health research projects using blockchain technology. Also, better public health research and sharing of data will lead to better care in many different industries. A central database is used to run the whole healthcare system and all the organisations that work with it.

Data security, sharing, and being able to work with other systems have been the biggest problems in population health management until now. Blockchain technology is a good answer for this situation. When used correctly, this technology improves access in real time, data exchange, interoperability, and data integrity. It also helps and encourages people to work together. Data security is very important, especially when it comes to wearable tech and personalised health care. Patients and medical professionals want an easy and safe way to get, send, and access data through networks without putting it at risk of being hacked. Blockchain technology is being used to solve these problems.

Blockchain Technology Supports Healthcare

Blockchain technology has many uses in the health care industry. Ledger technology helps researchers figure out genetic code by managing the supply chain for medicines, making sure the secure transmission of patient medical data, and making it easier to transfer patient medical records in a safe way. Figure 2 shows some of the different ways the Blockchain idea can be used, as well as some of the things that make it possible in a number of healthcare domains and industries. Some of the technical and impressive features used in the development and use of Blockchain technology are the protection of healthcare data, the management of different genomics, the management of electronic data, medical records, interoperability, digitalized tracking and issue outbreak, and other features like these. Blockchain technology is becoming more and more well-known. The main reasons for the widespread use of Blockchain technology are that all of its parts are completely digitalized and that it can be used in healthcare applications.

Benefits

When blockchain technology is used in the real world and solves problems in the healthcare industry, it can lead to a number of advantages and benefits. Here are some of these perks and benefits:

Continuous Keeping an Eye On

One of the most important things that the team in charge of running the healthcare network needs right now is strong oversight and monitoring of all kinds of transactions. Blockchain can keep track of all transactions in a decentralised ledger, which is something that standard healthcare administration systems can't do. This is what makes Blockchain different from other ways to manage healthcare. It saves time, effort, and money, and because it is accurate and clear at its core, you don't have to worry about managing it over time.

There is more cooperation than before.

The most important factor in the success of any healthcare-related project is the people involved, whether they are professionals, researchers, or other people. One way that blockchain technology makes it easier for the people listed above to connect and work together is by letting them use distributed ledger technology, which lets them give useful feedback and study together.

Safety of Information

From what we've talked about so far, it seems that the biggest problem facing the healthcare industry is the theft of important information and its use for bad reasons or other vested interests. A second part of the job is making sure that people who use the database can see the most up-to-date and correct patient information and diagnoses. This is an important part of the job. Blockchain technology can't be broken because it uses the best encryption methods. This lets the data be verified with a digital signature and protects it in a way that can't be broken. This helps trust and security concerns settle down in the long run.

Cheaper medication and fast processing

Setting up fast, streamlined, and high-quality data transmission and sharing across all important network members and healthcare experts helps to find new, cost-effective ways to treat and cure a wide range of diseases.

Blockchain assisted healthcare applications

BurstIQ

Location Denver, Colorado

With the technology that BurstIQ has made, healthcare organisations can handle a lot of patient information in a safe and secure way. It can store, sell, distribute, and licence data while still following HIPAA rules by using blockchain technology. The BurstIQ platform could help stop people from abusing opioids and other prescription drugs because it gives full and up-to-date information about people's health and healthcare activity.

doc.ai

Location:California

Machine Intelligence, which is similar to AI, is used by Doc ai to decentralise healthcare on the blockchain. Users can choose to use the company's platform to share their medical and genomic information with a community of scientists who use the information for predictive modelling. Doc.ai does not save any patient data. The data is erased after it is entered, encrypted on a blockchain, and used in a trial to make sure that it is kept private and secret.

Akiri

Location: California

Akiri runs a network-as-a-service for the healthcare industry that makes it easy to send health data about patients in a secure way. The Akiri system lacks storage for data. It works as both a network and a protocol to set up data layers, make rules, and instantly verify the sources and destinations of data. Akiri makes sure that medical information is safe and that only the right people can get to it when they need to.

Medicalchain

Location: London

The blockchain that Medicalchain uses creates a single source of truth and guarantees the veracity of medical records. Patients' identifiable and traceable information might be requested by doctors, hospitals, and laboratories.

Coral Health

Location: New York

Coral Health is using blockchain to improve patient outcomes, speed up administrative processes, and streamline customer service. The startup enables communication between doctors, scientists, lab workers, and public health officials easier than ever by linking patient data to distributed ledger technology. To ensure the accuracy of data and treatments, Coral Health also makes use of smart contracts between patients and doctors.

Avaneer Health

Location: Chicago

Avaneer is a company that uses blockchain technology to improve the efficiency of health care. It has the support of Aetna, Anthem, the Cleveland Clinic, and other well-known health care groups. Avaneer uses a public ledger to help with better claims processing, secure exchanges of health data, and up-to-date directories of providers.

Guardtime

Location:Switzerland

With the help of Guardtime, governments and healthcare organisations are adding blockchain to their cybersecurity plans. The company made a deal with a private healthcare provider in the UAE to use blockchain technology to keep its data private. The company had a big impact on how Estonia's health care institutions used blockchain technology.

References:
- *Haleem, M. Javaid, R. P. Singh, R. Suman, and S. Rab, "Blockchain technology applications in healthcare: An overview," International Journal of Intelligent Networks, vol. 2, pp. 130–139, 2021.*
- *H. Agarwal, "Benefits of using Blockchain technology in Healthcare," techexactly, 20-Jul-2020.*
- *S. Daley, "Blockchain in healthcare: 17 examples to know," Built In, 09-Aug-2022. [Online]. Available: https://builtin.com/blockchain/blockchain-healthcare-applications-companies.*

5. Blockchain in Supply Chain

Blockchain provides supply chain capabilities that were not possible in the recent past.

— Dave Waters

What does a supply chain mean?

Almost every product that people use is the result of the work of more than one group or organisation. All of them are part of the supply chain.

In a supply chain, the organisations are linked by the flow of goods and information:

- Physical flows include changing, moving, and storing materials and goods.

- Information flows include long-term planning and working with partners to manage the daily movement of materials and things along the supply chain.

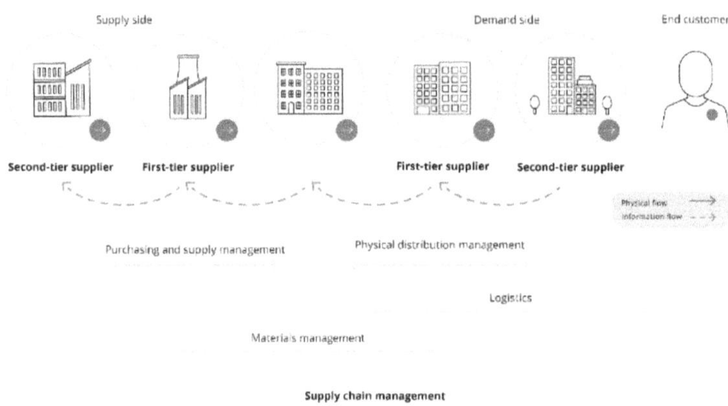

Figure 3:Simple Supplychain

Supply chain management is the process of ensuring that raw materials, completed goods, and products are moved from one place to another in the appropriate quantities and on schedule (SCM). A successful supply chain management strategy may reduce risk, speed up production, and reduce costs.

Problems in Supply Chain

One of the most important problems businesses face today is that the supply chain is not clear.

Alexis Bateman, who is in charge of MIT Sustainable Supply Chains at the MIT Center for Transportation and Logistics, says that supply chain openness is made up of two parts:

- Visibility: Seeing and getting information from every link in the supply chain.

- Disclosure: Making this information available to the right people inside and outside of the company.

Organizations must look at their industries, the laws that apply, their code of ethics, suppliers, consumers, past supply chain problems, and the level of risk they are willing to take when deciding how open their supply chain should be.

Another common issue is a system that doesn't work well, like when vendors and suppliers can't figure out who needs what, when, and how. Inefficiencies include poor management of upstream inventory, poor distribution of products to retailers, changing demand, and even slow shelf rotation. Product recalls are also expensive and take a lot of time because companies have to find suppliers and trace items back to their source to fix problems.

Blockchain based solution for supply chain

For organisations, the blockchain makes it easier and more secure to track all kinds of transactions. The supply chain can suffer a great deal. Businesses can utilise blockchain to find the origin and current location of a product. A secure transaction record is created each time a product is traded. By doing this, a permanent record of the item's creation through sale is produced.

- By utilising this cutting-edge technology, parties cooperating on a single platform might cut down on the regular transactional delays, unnecessary costs, and human blunders. Fraud is less likely when there are no middlemen in the supply chain. Finally, because businesses keep detailed records, they can trace the origins of fraud when it occurs.

- The flow of data, products, and money along a supply chain is tracked by a distributed blockchain record that cannot be changed. Using a shared blockchain, businesses can simply track shipments, make payments, and keep logistical data synchronised. They can continue to send only the most important information and they can do this without substantially altering their current processes.

- Businesses can deal with each other directly, without the help of a third party. This makes global supply chains more efficient. It also encourages the integration of financial and logistical services, which makes it easier for stakeholders to work together on data.

- Integrated payment systems shorten the time between placing an order and getting paid, which makes sure that goods are transported on time and correctly. Blockchain technology and smart contracts can also help businesses improve their compliance by reducing legal fees and penalties for late tax payments and getting rid of counterfeiting and fraud.

- Businesses can combine RFID tags, which use electromagnetic waves to identify and track objects, with blockchain technology. As supply chains get more automated, they are often used to collect information about products and prove when ownership or possession has changed hands. A smart contract is met when goods with RFID tags that have codes that can be automatically scanned arrive at their destination.

- Money may now be sent anywhere in the globe without going through a bank thanks to blockchain technology. Instead, transactions are carried out directly between the donors and recipients of payments. In addition, compared to days for transactions like automated clearing house payments, it is secure and quick, taking only minutes.Additionally, bitcoin transfer fees are lower. Some suppliers of the Australian carmaker Tomcar are paid in bitcoin. To pay its three partners in Taiwan and Israel, Tomcar is now using Bitcoin.

- Financial savings are an advantage. To prevent keeping an excessive amount of Bitcoin, the organisation takes steps. Despite the fact that Bitcoin is a global currency, some nations view it as a way for businesses to invest. Businesses might thus be required to pay taxes on their Bitcoin holdings.

- Traceability of meat Businesses can employ distributed ledger systems, also referred to as "blockchains," to track a product's status at every stage of production. There won't be any manipulation of the documents in any form. They make it possible to identify each object's origin. Using blockchain, the international corporation Walmart keeps track of how much pork is sold in China. The company's technology enables it to know the origin of each beef piece, the procedures needed to process and store it, and the ideal time to sell it. In the event of a recall, the business can also determine which batches were impacted and who made the purchases.

Businesses utilising blockchain in the supply chain

FedEx

It is one of the largest delivery companies in the world, is without a doubt one of the most important people pushing for an industry standard based on blockchain. The company has added blockchain technology to its custody chain to make it easier to find where something came from. This gives them a more reliable and effective way to deal with problems and questions from clients. Fedex started a pilot programme and joined the Blockchain in Transport Alliance, or BiTA, to make it clear what data should be stored on the blockchain and better meet customer expectations.

Nestle

The 150-year-old Swiss food giant has recently invested a substantial amount of time and money to increase the transparency of its supply chain. It has placed a great deal of faith in the potential of blockchain technology for this purpose. Nestlé is among the firms that contributed to the establishment of the IBM Food Trust. This SaaS platform provides users with access to vital food supply chain data, including a food item's complete history, current location, and any certifications, test results, and temperature data. In addition, the company is said to be the first big food and beverage company to test a blockchain platform in 2019 to increase supply chain transparency. Due to the company's partnership with OpenSC, customers can track the origin of the ingredients in their food, from the New Zealand milk to the American palm oil, all the way down to the farm. Another Amazon Managed Blockchain customer is Nestlé. The platform is used to monitor the complete production and supply chain process.

Ford Motor Company

Ford is using IBM's blockchain technology to make sure it gets cobalt in an ethical way. Cobalt is a key part of the batteries that power electric cars, but its mining causes a lot of damage to the environment. When cobalt is mined, Ford gets a book that it can use to keep track of its progress. (Ford is not the only one in this group. Volvo invests in the blockchain startup Circulor to track down cobalt in electric car batteries. Porsche works with Circularise to track down plastic on the blockchain. Ford also worked with other large manufacturers and the non-profit mobility alliance MOBI in 2017 to create supply chain standards for the automotive industry based on blockchain technology.

De Beers & Company

De Beers, one of the biggest diamond companies in the world, uses Tracr's blockchain-based tracking features to find out where each natural diamond it mines came from. Even though a lot is being done around the world to clean it up, diamond mining is still seen as dangerous and bad for the environment and the people who work there. De Beers uses Tracr to make sure that its diamonds are real and to make sure that its customers don't worry about the moral origin of its jewels by making sure that they don't come from war zones where they could be used to fund killing.

References:
- *A. Jara, "What is blockchain in supply chain management?," GetSmarter Blog, 11-Feb-2022. [Online]. Available: https://www.getsmarter.com/blog/market-trends/how-blockchain-will-radically-improve-the-supply-chain/.*
- *R. O'Byrne, "Applications of Blockchain in supply chain," Supply Chain Channel, 02-Mar-2020. [Online]. Available: https://supplychainchannel.co/applications-of-blockchain-in-supply-chain/.*
- *E. Glover, "5 uses of blockchain in the supply chain," Built In, 22-Sep-2022. [Online]. Available: https://builtin.com/blockchain/blockchain-in-supply-ch*